CORK CITY
HISTORY TOUR

Dedicated to my aunt, Ellie

Front cover image: South Gate Bridge, *c.* 1900. (Source: Cork City Library)
Back cover image: Blackrock Castle, *c.* 1930. (Source: Cork City Museum)

First published 2016

Amberley Publishing
The Hill, Stroud,
Gloucestershire, GL5 4EP
www.amberley-books.com

Copyright © Kieran McCarthy, 2016
Map contains Ordnance Survey data
© Crown copyright and database right
[2016]

The right of Kieran McCarthy to be
identified as the Author of this work
has been asserted in accordance with
the Copyrights, Designs and Patents
Act 1988.

ISBN 978 1 4456 6429 3 (print)
ISBN 978 1 4456 6430 9 (ebook)

All rights reserved. No part of this
book may be reprinted or reproduced
or utilised in any form or by any
electronic, mechanical or other means,
now known or hereafter invented,
including photocopying and recording,
or in any information storage or
retrieval system, without the permission
in writing from the Publishers.

British Library Cataloguing in
Publication Data.
A catalogue record for this book is
available from the British Library.

Map illustration by Thomas Bohm, User
Design Illustration and Typesetting.

Origination by Amberley Publishing.
Printed in Great Britain.

INTRODUCTION

They say the best way to get to know a city is to walk it. In Cork, you can get lost in narrow streets, marvel at old cobbled laneways, photograph old street corners, look up beyond the modern shopfronts, gaze at clues from the past, be enthused and at the same time disgusted by a view, smile at interested locals, engage in the forgotten and the remembered, search for and connect with something and thirst in the sense of storytelling – in essence, feel the DNA of the place.

Cork has a soul packed full of ambition and heart. Giving walking tours over twenty-one years has allowed me to bring people on a journey into that soul, but also receive feedback on the wider context of what visitors and locals have seen elsewhere. Cork is a city packed with historic gems, all waiting to be discovered at every street corner. This book provides insights into fifty such sites in and around the city centre island. One could have easily added three and four times as many sites to a book such as this.

Cork possesses a north-west European and an eastern North Atlantic port story. Located in the south of Ireland, it is windswept by tail ends of North Atlantic storms, which consistently drench the city, and rural areas with wind and rain, but they showcase a very photogenic urbanity with amazing sunsets on the river channels and a resilient green agricultural hinterland and chiselled raw coastline. Cork's former historic networks and contacts are reflected in the physical metropolitan fabric – its bricks, street layout and decaying timber wharfs. Inspired by other cities with similar trading partners, Cork forged its own unique take on port architecture.

Twice a day and every day, the tide sweeps in to erase part of this history. The river meanders through this city and sweeps its historic narratives along. Cork is as bound to the river and tide as they are bound to it. It developed because of its connections through water to other cities in Ireland and within the former British Empire. Exploring the harbour area, one can still find residues of the mudflat, estuarine silt landscape that the city was constructed upon. It is a great feat of engineering to build a city on a swamp.

The first known settlement at Cork began as a monastic centre in the seventh century, founded by St Fin Barre. This is now marked by the late nineteenth-century structure of St Fin Barre's Cathedral. It stands tall and proud in its ecclesiastical heritage, also imbuing the city and wider region with a need for community and to invest physically and morally in such structures. Hence, Cork has a myriad of church buildings with different styles from different times when such buildings were called upon to impart new messages about their contribution to the city.

The main urban centre was built on a series of marshy islands at the lowest crossing point of the river, where it meets the sea. One can imagine the timber posts struck into the marshland to mark out the tentative first couple of Viking houses, and the first fires lit in such flood-prone structures. The Vikings were the first to develop a basic bridge spanning from the valley side to the marsh, now marked by South Gate Bridge. This was the start of a rich maritime history and a strong identification as a port town.

The laying of the first block of the Anglo-Norman town wall must have been equally momentous. The actual stone from beneath the encircling southern and northern hills – sandstone and limestone – provided the defences. The opening of Watergate for the first time and the control by King's Castle and Queen's Castle would have sparked excitement, especially as the first timber ship clocked against the quay walls. Similarly, the first ship from somewhere abroad in England or France would have brought a sense of wonder and acknowledgement in the city's role in maritime Western Europe.

The topping out of St Anne's Church, Shandon, and years later the addition of the bells and clocks, would have been met with delight and pride. From the top of Shandon, you can gaze down upon the multicoloured and multifaceted narrative presented in its urban fabric. Climbing down and walking among the streets and laneways and unravelling those narratives has brought great joy to me personally and has kept me with my camera and notebook in hand, trying to make sense of Cork's place in north-west Europe as an ambitious and soulful place. Enjoy the tour!

Kieran McCarthy

Cork City History Tour Key

1. University College Cork
2. Crawford College of Art & Design
3. St Fin Barre's Cathedral
4. Keyser's Hill
5. Elizabeth Fort
6. St Nicholas Church
7. Red Abbey
8. South Chapel
9. South Gate Bridge
10. An Upturned Cannon
11. Bishop Lucey Park
12. Courthouse
13. Watergate
14. St Peter's Church
15. North Gate Bridge
16. Butter Market
17. St. Anne's Church
18. Skiddy's Almshouse
19. St Mary and Anne's North Cathedral
20. Religious Sisters of Charity
21. Rebellions, Burning and Rebuilding
22. The Savoy
23. Cork's General Post Office
24. Cork Opera House
25. Crawford Municipal Art Gallery
26. The Canova Casts

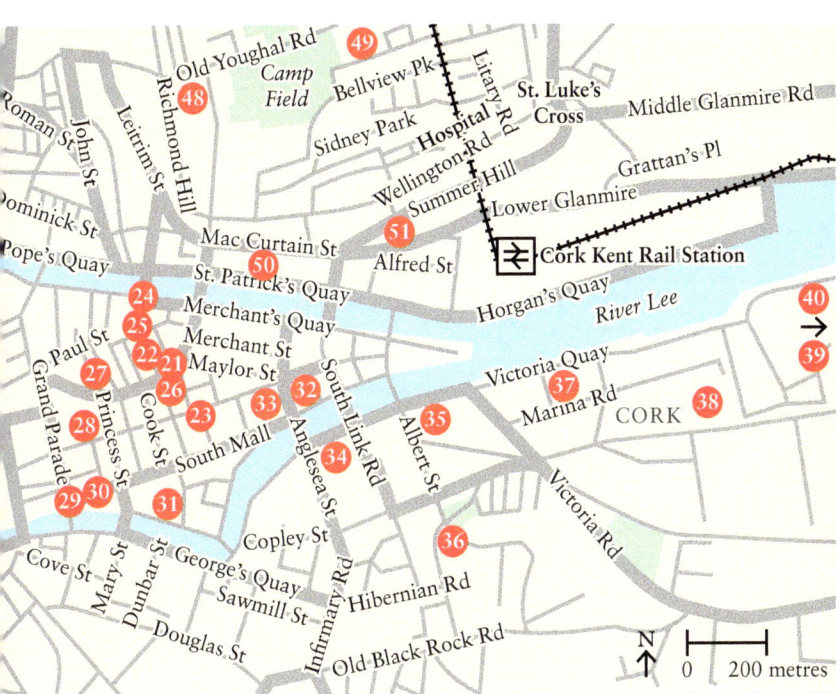

- 27 St Peter and Paul's Church
- 28 English Market
- 29 National Monument
- 30 First World War Memorial
- 31 Holy Trinity Church
- 32 Cork Savings Bank
- 33 Provincial Bank
- 34 Cork City Hall
- 35 Cork Blackrock & Passage Railway Line
- 36 Gasworks
- 37 Docks
- 38 Ford's Works
- 39 The Marina
- 40 Blackrock Castle
- 41 Mercy Hospital
- 42 Wise's Distillery
- 43 St Vincent's Church
- 44 Cork City Gaol
- 45 Daly's Bridge
- 46 Sunday's Well Boating and Tennis Club
- 47 Lifetime Lab
- 48 Audley Place
- 49 Collins Barracks
- 50 Metropole Hotel
- 51 St Patrick's Church

TRAIL WALKS

These Cork hotspots can be enjoyed in the listed trails or in one tour of the city.

Early Origins
Nos 1–8

This is a corner of Cork filled with iconic histories, which defined the early history of Cork and instilled into the urban space cultural narratives of legacies of monks, Viking marauders and English plantation fortresses. It is also the home of University College Cork, Crawford College of Art and St Marie's of the Isle. Education and learning play a huge part in this quadrant of the city. Scramble up Barrack Street and explore its multiple laneways, many dating back over 400 years, all adding immense historic character into the urban landscape.

Across the Medieval Core
Nos 9–15

In its day, the walled town of Cork would have dominated the swampy estuary of the River Lee. Imagine an 8- to 10-metre-high and 2-metre-wide rubble wall of limestone and sandstone, creaking drawbridges, mud-filled main streets and laneways, as well as timber- and stone-built dwellings complete with falling rood straw and a smoky atmosphere from lit house fires keeping out the damp. Today, one can still rediscover several of the later incarnations of structures marking medieval churches, tower houses and entrances.

Shandon
Nos 16–20

The Shandon Quarter was the northern suburb of the city in medieval times where those not willing to pay the property taxes lived. A tight-knit community, it witnessed the development of economic drivers for the city in the eighteenth and nineteenth centuries. Once the home of the city's cattle butcheries, the Butter Market and the spin-off industries of both, thousands of people were employed here. The area is home to some of Cork's historic landmarks, from Protestant St Anne's Church and graveyard to the beautiful interior of St Mary's and St Anne's Roman Catholic Cathedral.

St Patrick's Street
Nos 21–31

The curving St Patrick's Street was once a channel of the River Lee. In the eighteenth century, it became the central canal in the showcasing of the new city that was emerging. Today, the street and its surroundings have many historical highlights, from the Father Mathew statue to stories of Huguenots, churches, old cinemas and iconic monuments. Plus, why not do some shopping along the way or pick up a coffee or food in the beautiful English Market?

City Hall
Nos 32–40

Cork City Hall and docklands represent the ambition of the port city. These are places where conversations were had on Cork's place in the international network of port cities and places where the city's future was spoken about and planned for. Enjoy the walk around the beautiful 1930s city hall, the old docklands warehouses and the extensive Marina walk. Also, check out the legacies of the great industries of Ford and Dunlop's.

Western Quarter
Nos 41–47

An impressive historical quadrant of the city, this area showcases the best of eighteenth-century Cork, from the flat Mardyke walk to the architectural splendour of Sunday's Well. Splice in buildings such as the former mayoral residence, old distillery buildings and the City Gaol heritage centre, and they all add up to a strong sense of history and identity.

Ascending the North-East
Nos 48–51

This is a part of the city more affectionately described as the Victorian Quarter. The visitor can climb to the top of the city's steepest hill to capture the view down onto the flat of the city. Drop down from the hill onto Wellington Road and MacCurtain Street and learn about some of the city's beautiful redbrick- and limestone-clad structures. At every corner, there is another aspect of the city's heritage stock to discover.

University College, Cork.

EARLY ORIGINS

1. UNIVERSITY COLLEGE CORK

The origins of University College Cork (UCC) is linked to the legend of St Fin Barre who is reputed to have founded a monastery on and near this site around AD 600. Fast-forward to the modern day and UCC still harnesses the legend by extolling the motto, 'Where Finbarr taught, let Munster learn.' UCC was founded under the provisions made by Queen Victoria to endow new colleges in Ireland for the advancement of learning. Architects Benjamin Woodward and Sir Thomas Deane adopted a perpendicular Gothic style. The college opened on 7 November 1849 and was constructed at the height of the Irish Great Famine.

In 1908, the Queen's College, Cork, was established as a National University of Ireland under the 1908 constitution. Check out its Ogham Stone Corridor in the north wing, the wonderful Crawford Observatory and the Lewis Glucksman Art Gallery.

2. CRAWFORD COLLEGE OF ART & DESIGN

In May 1908, the local government board sanctioned the appointment of Arthur Hill of Cork as architect for a new technical institute building. However, the architect had no site to work from. Difficulties were experienced by the technical instruction committee in obtaining a suitable site, which were not overcome until early February 1909 when Arthur Frederick Sharman Crawford presented the former site of Arnott's Brewery on Fitton Street to the committee. Arthur Hill was the architect of many important buildings, such as the additions to the North Infirmary, the Victoria Buildings, the Cork Examiner Printing Works, as well as many shops in Cork and the country towns, and designed numerous pretty villas in Cork and its hinterland. The science laboratories at University College Cork, the Cork Municipal Technical Institute and the Munster and Leinster Bank were his chief works previous to the war.

3. ST FIN BARRE'S CATHEDRAL

St Fin Barre's Cathedral is another marker of the once-vibrant early Christian monastery. The eighteenth-century church was a plain classical building retaining the original tower of the first church. It was taken down in 1865 to make way for, in the words of the Bishop of Cork at the time, 'a structure more worthy of the name Cork Cathedral'. In 1863, a general committee arranged a competition to find an architect., and the unanimous winner was London-born William Burges, who whose interests in medieval Gothic architecture are apparent within the building, inspired by Notre Dame and Cologne. Check out the Golden Angel, which, according to legend, if she blows her trumpets – or falls off or turns green – the world is supposed to come to an end.

4. KEYSER'S HILL

The advent of Norwegian and Danish Vikings, in AD 820 and *c*. AD 914 respectively, marked the early origins of Cork as a port. These new invaders started by raiding the monastery, soon turning their attention to neighbouring powerful and wealthy political kingdoms in Munster. One such kingdom was Fir Maige. It is known that a Danish settlement area was located south of Fin Barre's monastery on the southern hillside, extending from what is now the present-day French's Quay and Barrack Street area to George's Quay. There is still Viking place name evidence in Keyser's Hill, which is Scandinavian, meaning 'the path leading to the quayside'.

5. ELIZABETH FORT

Constructed in 1601 by order of Elizabeth I, the star-shaped fortification once protected an English garrison in Cork and became a distinct landmark in the immediate southern suburbs. Named after the queen, it was an irregular fortification with stone walls on three sides and an earthen bank facing the town, protecting Cork from attack by Gaelic Irish natives and Spanish invasion. In the nineteenth century, the barracks within Elizabeth Fort were converted into a female prison and then used as a station for the Cork City Artillery Militia. In 1920–21, it was occupied by the Royal Irish Constabulary and handed over to the Provisional Irish government. None of the original fort can be seen today. Elizabeth Fort remains one of Cork's most historic gems. Never excavated, the old fort has a wealth of stories waiting to be discovered. Check out the tour and view from the ramparts.

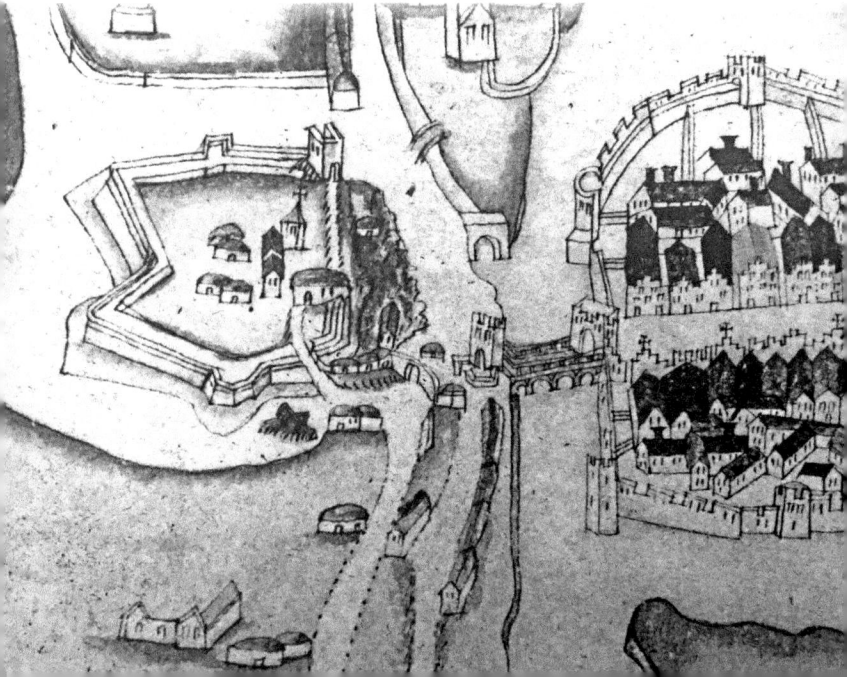

6. ST NICHOLAS' CHURCH

St Nicholas' Church was erected initially in honour of the Anglo-Norman victory over the Danish settlers in Cork in AD 1174. The Anglo-Norman church of St Nicholas was registered by its clergy in 1270 and granted by the Bishop of Cork to St Thomas's Abbey, Dublin. Nearly 400 years later, this church had stood the test of time. Severe damage was caused to St Nicholas' Church during the Williamite Siege of Cork in 1690 when Jacobite supporters occupied the walled town. It was only in 1720 when funds were allocated by the Protestant Bishop of Cork, Peter Browne, that a new St Nicholas' Church was built. Indeed, the finance for its construction came from the taxing of coal that was imported into Cork for domestic purposes.

In recent years, the probation service have appropriated the church for their offices. Check out the church's Tracton family monument in the Crawford Art Gallery.

7. RED ABBEY

The central bell tower of Red Abbey is a relic of the Anglo-Norman colonisation, one of the last remaining visible structures that date to the era of the walled town of Cork. Invited to Cork by the Anglo-Normans, the Augustinians established an abbey from 1270 to 1288, which was dedicated to the Most Holy Trinity but had several names. In the mid-eighteenth century, parts of Red Abbey were used a sugar refinery – this was accidentally burnt down in December 1799. Since then, the friary buildings, with the exception of the tower, have survived in piecemeal form.

8. SOUTH CHAPEL

The present South Chapel is the fourth on the site. The first existed in 1635 and was ruined by 1702. Around 1702, the second thatched church was built near Douglas Street in the precincts of the South Presentation Monastery – it was burned in 1727. On the same site, the third church was built in 1728. The present building was built in 1766 by Daniel O'Brien, OP, who was parish priest. The South Chapel was built in the Georgian style. The altar contains the *Dead Christ* sculpture by John Hogan (1806–70), the noted Irish sculptor. The Crucifixion, behind the altar, is said to have been painted by Cork artist John O'Keefe.

ACROSS THE MEDIEVAL CORE
9. SOUTH GATE BRIDGE

In the time of the Anglo-Normans establishing a fortified walled settlement and a trading centre in Cork around AD 1200, South Gate drawbridge formed one of the three entrances – North Gate Bridge and Watergate being the others. South Gate drawbridge was a wooden structure and was annually subjected to severe winter flooding, being almost destroyed in each instance.

In May 1711, agreement was reached by the council of the city that North Gate Bridge would be rebuilt in stone in 1712 while, in 1713, South Gate Bridge would be replaced with stone arched structures. Both North and South Gate drawbridges were designed and built by George Coltsman, a Cork City stonemason and architect. South Gate Bridge still stands today in its past form as it did over 300 years ago, apart from a small bit of restructuring and strengthening in early 1994.

10. AN UPTURNED CANNON

In September 1690, a Jacobite army, along with Irish rebel factions, combined forces to take control of Cork, providing a stronghold position against King William. They manned the drawbridges and the town wall walks and waited for the attack they knew must come. King William despatched the Earl of Marlborough to regain control. On 22 September 1690, Marlborough arrived in Cork Harbour with over eighty ships and approximately 5,000 men. Marlborough decided that he could exploit the main defensive disadvantage of the walled area: its low-lying position overlooked by hills. On 27 September, the cannons concentrated on breaching the eastern wall, a point now marked by the library. After a few more days, the rebels surrendered and the leaders were transported to the Tower of London.

11. BISHOP LUCEY PARK

In 1984–85, Bishop Lucey Park was created to celebrate the 800th anniversary of the first charter given by Henry II to the citizens of Cork. Ironically, while preparing the ground for the park, a section of the imposing town wall was revealed. In general, much of the town wall survives beneath the modern street surface of the city and in some places has been incorporated into the foundations of existing buildings, especially in those overlooking the Grand Parade. Initially created by the Anglo-Normans around AD 1180, the town walls were extended and rebuilt through subsequent centuries up to the Siege of Cork in 1690. Cork was one of fifty-eight walled towns in Ireland.

12. COURTHOUSE

In 1829, it was decided by Cork Corporation that both the city and county courthouses should be incorporated into one building, to be located on the new Great Georges Street on the old western line of the town wall. Designed by George Pain, the courthouse was built on the western line of the old town wall and opened in 1835. Years later, on Good Friday 27 March 1891, the interior was completely

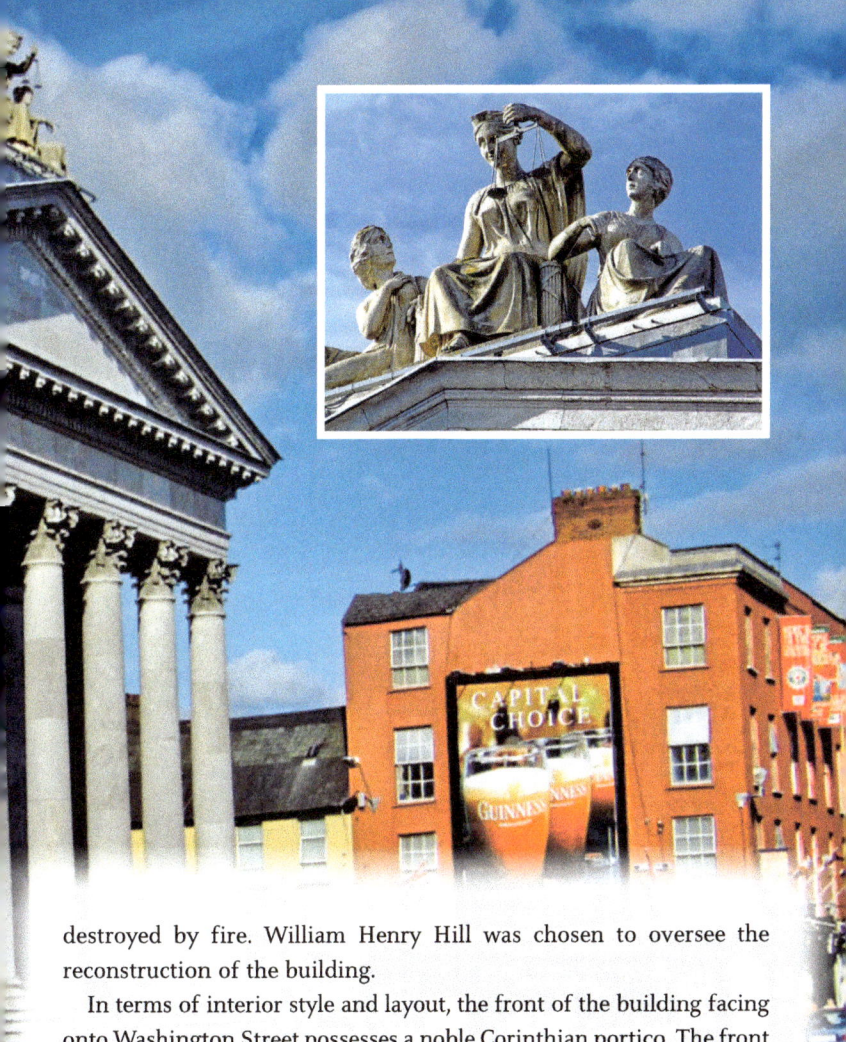

destroyed by fire. William Henry Hill was chosen to oversee the reconstruction of the building.

In terms of interior style and layout, the front of the building facing onto Washington Street possesses a noble Corinthian portico. The front range of Corinthian columns projects nearly 6 metres from the main building. The pillars are nearly 10 metres high. The impressive group of figures, which stand over the building, represent justice, law and mercy.

13. WATERGATE

The Watergate complex, comprising Cork's medieval port, docks and custom house, would have been impressive. The gate allowed controlled access into a private world of merchants and citizens – the masts of ships, vessels filled with goods and people, creaking as their wooden hulls knocked against the stone quays. Built between two marshy islands in the middle of a walled town, its entrance was between the two castles – King's Castle and Queen's Castle. King's and Queen's Castles are signified in the city's coat of arms with a ship travelling from one tower to another and the Latin inscription, '*Statio Bene Fida Carinis*', which means 'A Safe Harbour for Ships.' In the late thirteenth century, Cork had 17 per cent of all Irish trade and was the third most important port in Ireland after New Ross and Waterford. Trading was also conducted between Cork and Bristol, Chichester, Minehead, Southampton and Portsmouth.

14. ST PETER'S CHURCH

Overlooking North Main Street, present-day St Peter's Church is the second church to be built on its site. The first church was built sometime in the early fourteenth century. In 1782, the church was taken down and in 1783, the present limestone walled church was begun to be built. In recent years, St Peter's Church has been extensively renovated and opened as an arts exhibition centre. One of the most interesting monuments on display in the church is the Deane monument. This monument, dating to 1710, was dedicated to the memory of Sir Matthew Deane and his wife and both are depicted on the monument, shown in solemn prayer on both sides of an altar tomb.

15. NORTH GATE BRIDGE

As the northern access route into the walled town, North Gate drawbridge was a wooden structure and was annually subjected to severe winter flooding, being almost destroyed in each instance. In May 1711, agreement was reached by the council of the city that North Gate Bridge be rebuilt in stone in 1712 while, in 1713, South Gate Bridge would be replaced with a stone arched structure. The new North and South Gate bridges were designed and built by George Coltsman.

Between 1713 and the early 1800s, the only structural work completed on North Gate Bridge was the repairing and widening of it by the Corporation of Cork. It was in 1831 that they saw the structure was deteriorating and deemed it unsafe as a river crossing for horses, carts, and coaches. Hence, in October 1861, the plans by

Cork architect Sir John Benson for a new bridge were accepted.

In April 1863, the foundation stone for the new bridge was laid. The new bridge was to be a cast-iron structure with the ironwork completed by Ranking & Co. of Liverpool. An ornate Victorian style was incorporated into the new structure with features such as ornamental lamp posts and iron medallions depicting Queen Victoria, Albert, the Prince Consort, Daniel O'Connell, the Irish 'Liberator' and Sir Thomas Moore, the famous English poet. On 6 November 1961, the new and present-day bridge was opened by Lord Mayor, Antony Barry TD. The new bridge was named Griffith Bridge in honour of Arthur Griffith who was a famous republican politician in Ireland in the early 1920s.

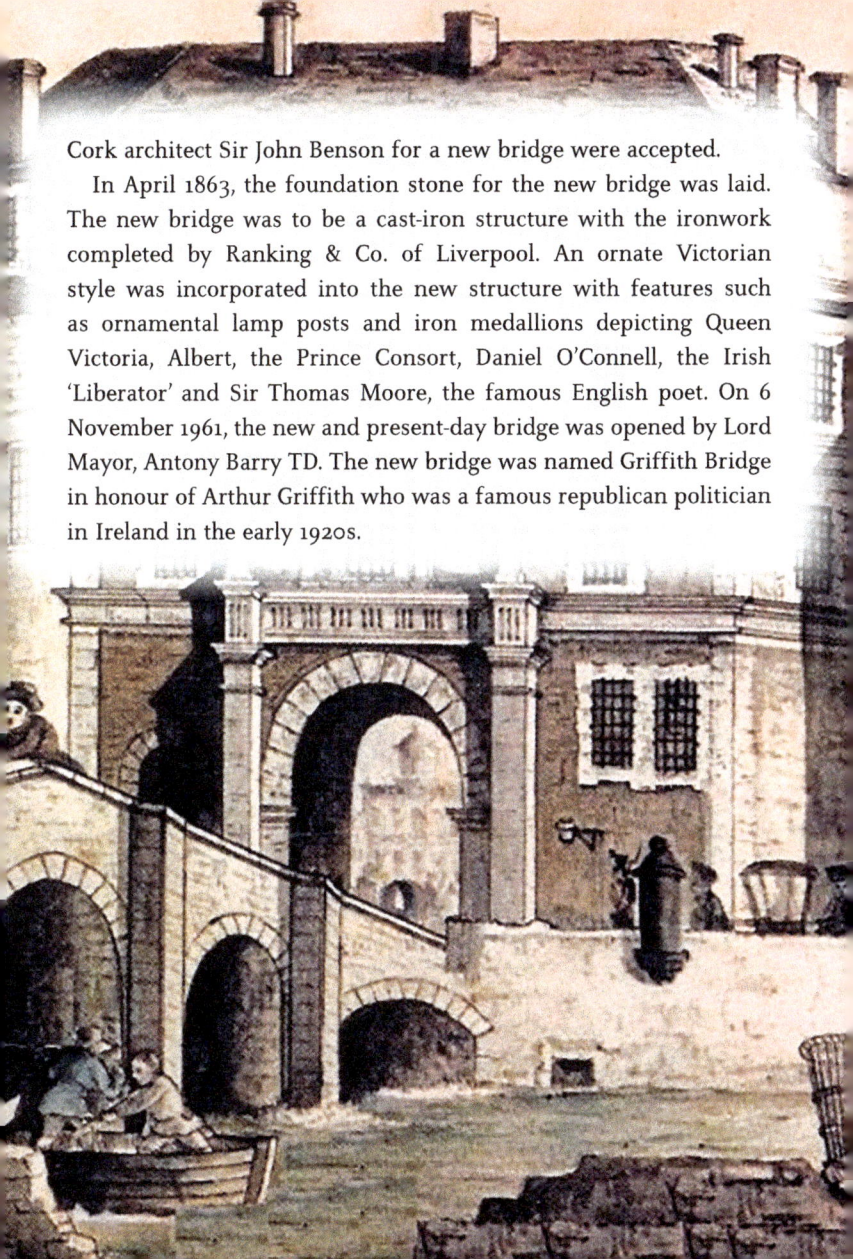

SHANDON
16. BUTTER MARKET

By the mid-eighteenth century, the native butter industry in Cork, based in Shandon, had grown to such an extent that it was decided among the main city and county butter merchants that an institution be established in the city that would control and develop its potential – the 'Committee of Butter Merchants'. In May 1770, it was decided by the twenty-one members of the committee that all butter to be exported from Cork was to be examined by appointed inspectors. On examination of the casks, the quality of butter was determined and they were awarded a 'first', 'second', 'third', 'fourth', 'fifth', or 'sixth'.

17. ST ANNE'S CHURCH

The name Shandon comes from the Irish word '*Sean Dún*', which means 'old fort' and it is said to mark the ring fort of the Irish family MacCarthaigh, who lived in the area around AD 1,000. St Anne's, Shandon, was built in 1722 to replace the older and local church of St Mary's, which was destroyed in the siege of Cork in 1690 by English forces. In 1750, the firm of Abel Rudhall in Gloucester cast the famous bells of Shandon. On 7 December 1752, the bells were first used and were rung in celebration and recognition of the marriage of Mr Henry Harding to Miss Catherine Dorman. Inscriptions can be found on the bells, which contain messages of joy and death. Above three tiers is an ornamental gold-coloured gilt ball and a weathervane in the form of a fish. The giant glided fish, 4–5 metres in length, is a very relevant sign to have in a church, as in the earliest days of Christianity a fish was used as a symbol for the name of Christ. The clock of Shandon was installed by Cork Corporation in 1847. It was made by James Mangan, a successful Cork watchmaker.

18. SKIDDY'S ALMSHOUSE

Financial support to the less fortunate citizens of Cork – both Catholic and Protestant – was much needed in the early eighteenth century. In 1715, the Green Coat Hospital was built on a waste piece of ground adjoining the churchyard of St Mary's Church, Shandon. Revd Dr Henry Maule presented the ground to the trustees of the hospital for development. Thomas Newnham, a Cork merchant and Quaker, financially subscribed to the completion of the project. In March 1715, construction commenced on further wasteland given by Revd Maule adjacent to the Green Coat Hospital to construct two schools. Any citizens interested in attending had to be of Protestant belief. Boys were to be taught reading, writing and accounts while girls were to be taught to read, knit, sew and spin. On the entrance to the schools were statues of a boy and girl. In true Cork fashion, the statues were named, Bob and Joan and are now housed in the steeple of St Anne's Church, Shandon.

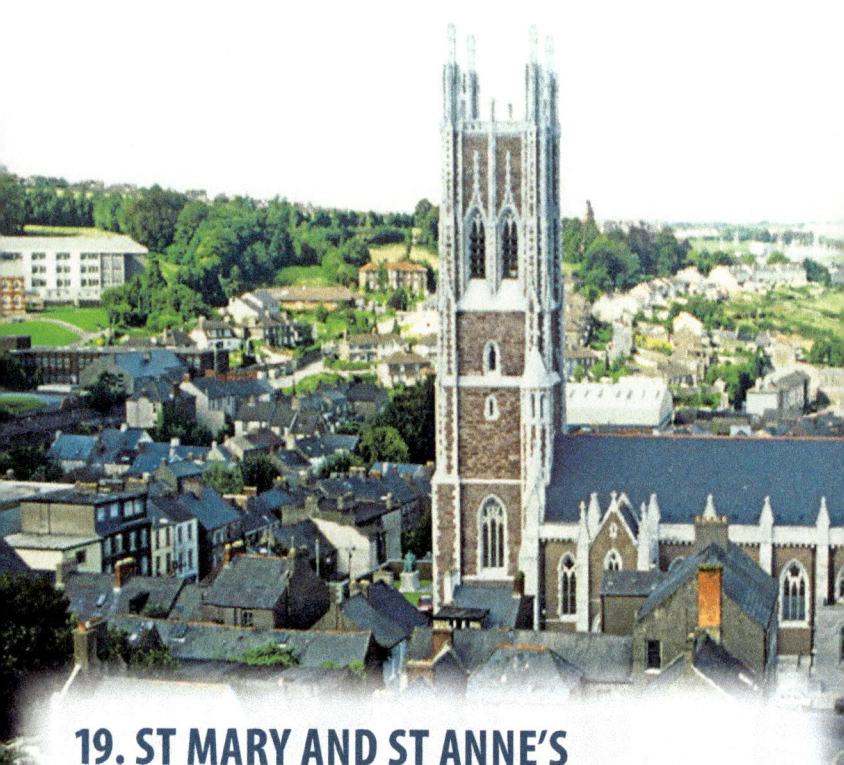

19. ST MARY AND ST ANNE'S NORTH CATHEDRAL

The present Cathedral of St Mary's and St Anne's is the fifth church on the site since the early 1600s. In 1820, an immense fire greatly damaged the fourth cathedral so much so that it was really the skeleton structure of the burned cathedral that survived. However, all was not lost and, shortly after, the bishop of that time, John Murphy, delegated the rebuilding of the then twelve-year-old cathedral to architect George Pain, who was also responsible for the design of buildings such as Holy Trinity Church, St Patrick's Church and Blackrock Castle.

In 1868, at an influential meeting of Catholic citizens, convened by the Bishop of Cork and Cloyne, Delany, certain alterations and improvements to the church were debated. Early work commenced on the rebuilding of the buttresses, rearrangement of the windows, and addition of the parapet and minarets to the southern aisle of the nave. However, this was when the project ran into financial difficulty and the remaining features of Benson's proposals were never carried out. Instead of the proposed spire, four pinnacles were designed and constructed.

20. RELIGIOUS SISTERS OF CHARITY

In the first decade of the 1800s, the Catholic Bishop of Cork, Francis Moylan, wished to answer the needs of the poor in the city. He was anxious for religious orders to establish themselves in the urban area. In the early 1820s, his successor, Bishop Murphy, was to invite Cork-born Mother Mary Aikenhead and her order, the Religious Sisters of Charity, to Cork. Five Sisters of Charity, along with Mother Mary Aikenhead, came to Cork in 1826. The dwelling, which Bishop Murphy had selected for the community, was a damp, gloomy and tumbledown house. It stood close to the North Cathedral in the poorest quarter of the city.

On 19 November 1826, the sisters began the formal visitation of the poor in the North Parish. Typhus fever was raging and the wretched slum area visited by the nuns was a hotbed of infection. They distributed tickets for food and coal, which were placed at their disposal by city officers of health. The sisters also gave religious instruction in the North Infirmary. At the Bishop's request, the sisters visited a local refuge for women, which had been founded in 1809 by the financial support of prominent city merchant, Nicholas Terry, and was then under secular control. The refuge accommodated thirteen young women when, on 8 June 1846, at the request of the bishop, the sisters took charge of the institution. Two years previously, a larger convent, named St Vincent's, was built in Peacock Lane, very near to Eason's Hill in the Shandon area. The sisters opened an infant school near this site in 1857. This was later followed by primary and secondary schools.

ST PATRICK'S STREET
21. REBELLIONS, BURNING AND REBUILDING

Two styles of architecture grace St Patrick's Street, the northern side comprising the nineteenth-century style while the southern side comprises the early twentieth-century style. The latter is the result of Ireland's War of Independence in 1920. In response to Irish Republican activities in Cork, and in the country as a whole, from January 1920 the British government increased the number of men serving in the Royal Irish Constabulary, recruiting the infamous Black and Tans. The total number of British government servants in Ireland came to approximately 40,000, while the IRA numbered 5,000 men. Thus, more often than not, the Irish Republican Army employed hit-and-run tactics.

In December 1920, six IRA men ambushed a troupe of auxiliaries within 100 metres of the central military barracks near Dillion's Cross on the north side of Cork City. At least one auxiliary was killed and twelve others wounded. In retaliation, indiscriminate shooting commenced by the auxiliaries and Black and Tans in the main city centre streets shortly after eight o'clock. Fires spread rapidly and soon most of the southern side of St Patrick's Street was ablaze. Cork City Hall and the adjacent Andrew Carnegie Library were destroyed, with large tracts of Cork's public and historic records destroyed forever.

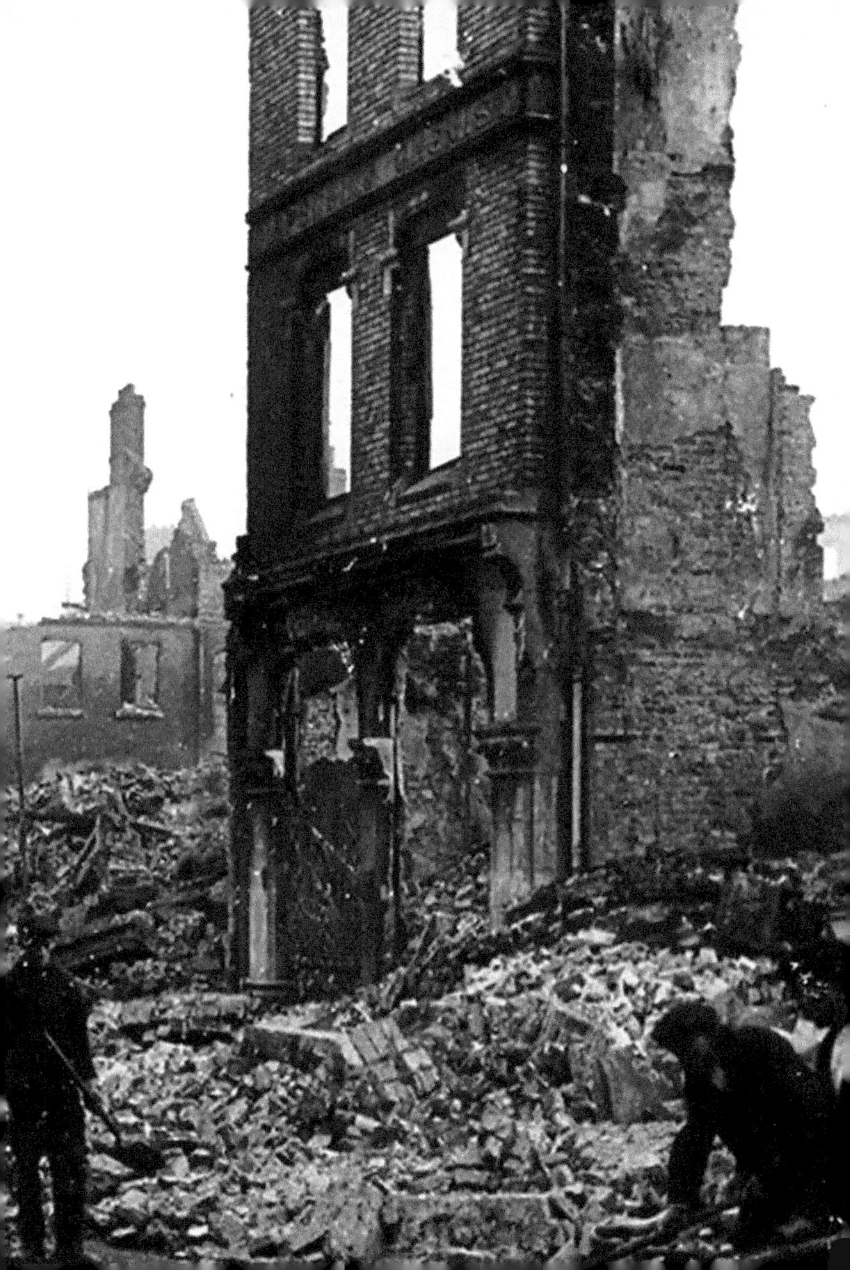

22. THE SAVOY

Two fine places of entertainment, two cinemas of high repute, the Savoy and the Pavillion adorned St Patrick's Street for much of the twentieth century. The Savoy cinema was constructed in the early 1930s, was commissioned by the Rank Organisation, and was built by the firm Meagher & Hayes. The first film was shown on Thursday 12 May 1932. The cinema had a colourful art deco exterior with an imposing exterior-lighted canopy. The interior design was elaborate with a spacious marble foyer. The rear of the Grand Circle was known as 'the

SAVOY CINEMA

WE HAD THE PRIVILEGE OF SUPPLYING THE UNIFORMS FOR THE USHERESSES, WAITRESSES AND PAGETTES. THESE GARMENTS WERE MADE ENTIRELY IN OUR OWN WORKROOMS.

Dowdens
Patrick St CORK

Gods', which was the cheapest part of the house. The grand auditorium held an audience of 2,249 patrons. The Studios of Rank, United Artists, 20th Century Fox and Columbia supplied new films to the Savoy and the programme changed twice a week on Sundays and Wednesdays.

Sunday was always *the* night of the week to go to the pictures. The general public dressed in their best clothes. Fred Bridgeman, the organist, was the Savoy's top live entertainer for nearly thirty years. The Cork Film International Festival, originally called 'An Tóstal', began in 1953.

23. CORK'S GENERAL POST OFFICE

With increasing wealth in the city came a proposal in 1759 by the management of the Crow Street Theatre Dublin, headed by Presario Spranger Barry, to create a playhouse fitting of Ireland's second city. The new building was located three blocks east of the old Theatre Royal on the same side of George's Street between Morgan's Lane (now Morgan Street) and Five Alley Lane (now Pembroke Street). The Cork General Post Office now occupies the site. The playhouse façade on George's Street possessed a ground-floor arcade or a façade similar to that of the Crow Street.

A fire gutted the Theatre Royal in 1840, but it was reopened in 1853. In 1875, owner James Scanlan sold the Cork Theatre Royal on Oliver Plunkett Street to the postal authorities, who were to use the building as the city's general post office. On 10 April 1875, the last three professional performances that were to take place in the Theatre Royal were announced in the *Cork Examiner*. These performances comprised; Monday 11 April, *Virginius*; Tuesday 12 April, *Hamlet*; Wednesday 13 April, *Belpheggar*. After a period of 113 years, from 1760 to 1875, Cork Theatre Royal manager James Scanlan shifted the centre of theatrical interest to a building at the side of the northern branch of the River Lee, which had been variously known as the Athenaeum – the city's arts venue.

24. CORK OPERA HOUSE

The fabric of the Athenaeum was from the Cork National Exhibition Hall of 1852. As a lecture and assembly hall, the uses of the Athenaeum were limited and, in 1874, when the ownership of the building came into the hands of James Scanlan, he remodelled it and added a 700-seat concert hall. In addition, he changed the name to the Munster Hall or Halls. Remodelling made stage performances far more practical but the premises was more suited to concerts. In 1875, a group of citizens, under the chairmanship of Mr John George McCarthy, MP and local historian, formed the Great and Royal Opera House Co. and purchased the Munster Hall from Scanlan. Indeed, at the same time, music as a cultural element in the city began to be developed on a professional level. Opera was hugely popular among Corkonians. On 17 September 1877, Cork Opera House opened its doors to begin its long illustrious career as Cork's principal theatre. Mr C. J. Phipps of London was commissioned to design the Cork Opera House.

James Scanlan operated under a board of directors acting on behalf of a private limited company. However, the company that was formed in 1877 went into liquidation in 1888. A fresh group of enthusiasts formed a new company with a capital of £12,000 and this was the company, which, through all the trials and tribulations, was still in existence when the theatre burned down in 1955. Cork Opera House was reopened with a new look in October 1965, with further renovations in the early twenty-first century.

School of Art and Opera House, Cork.

25. CRAWFORD MUNICIPAL ART GALLERY

In 1883, a deputation, consisting of Mr James Brenan, RHA, schoolmaster of the Cork School of Art and the honorary secretary, was sent to London to request further finance from Mr Mundella, the then vice president of the Committee of Council for Education, for finance to construct a municipal art gallery. Several months later, through the efforts of the committee and headmaster James Brenan, William Horatio Crawford, a prominent Cork City merchant, decided to donate the necessary finance to complete a renovation and extension of the existing School of Art. The cost was £20,000 and Arthur Hill of the architect firm of Hill & Co. designed the renovated building and extension. It was originally proposed that the extension and additions would include a School of Art and Science and the wrought-iron gates visible today at the entrance to the Crawford Art Gallery still bear the inscriptions 'Art' and 'Science'.

26. THE CANOVA CASTS

In the second decade of the 1800s, the acquisition of the classical casts of Antonio Canova was an important contribution to the cultural status of Cork. Circa 1810, Pope Pius VII was anxious to express his gratitude to the English people for the return to the Vatican Galleries of many masterpieces looted by Napoleon Bonaparte. Thus, the Pope commissioned Italian artist Antonio Canova to make a set of over 100 casts from the classical collection in the Vatican. In 1812, the casts were shipped to London as a gift to the Prince Regent, later

George IV. The prince showed a lack of appreciation towards his papal acquisitions and they lay firstly in the London Custom House and then in the basement of his residence in Carleton Gardens. Lord Listowel of Convamore, County Cork, a patron of the arts and a friend of the prince, suggested that they should be donated as a gift to the people of Cork. Agreeing, the prince donated them to the Society of Fine Arts in the city, whose premises was located on the intersection of St Patrick's Street and Falkener's Lane. In contemporary terms, several of the casts can be viewed today in the Crawford Art Gallery.

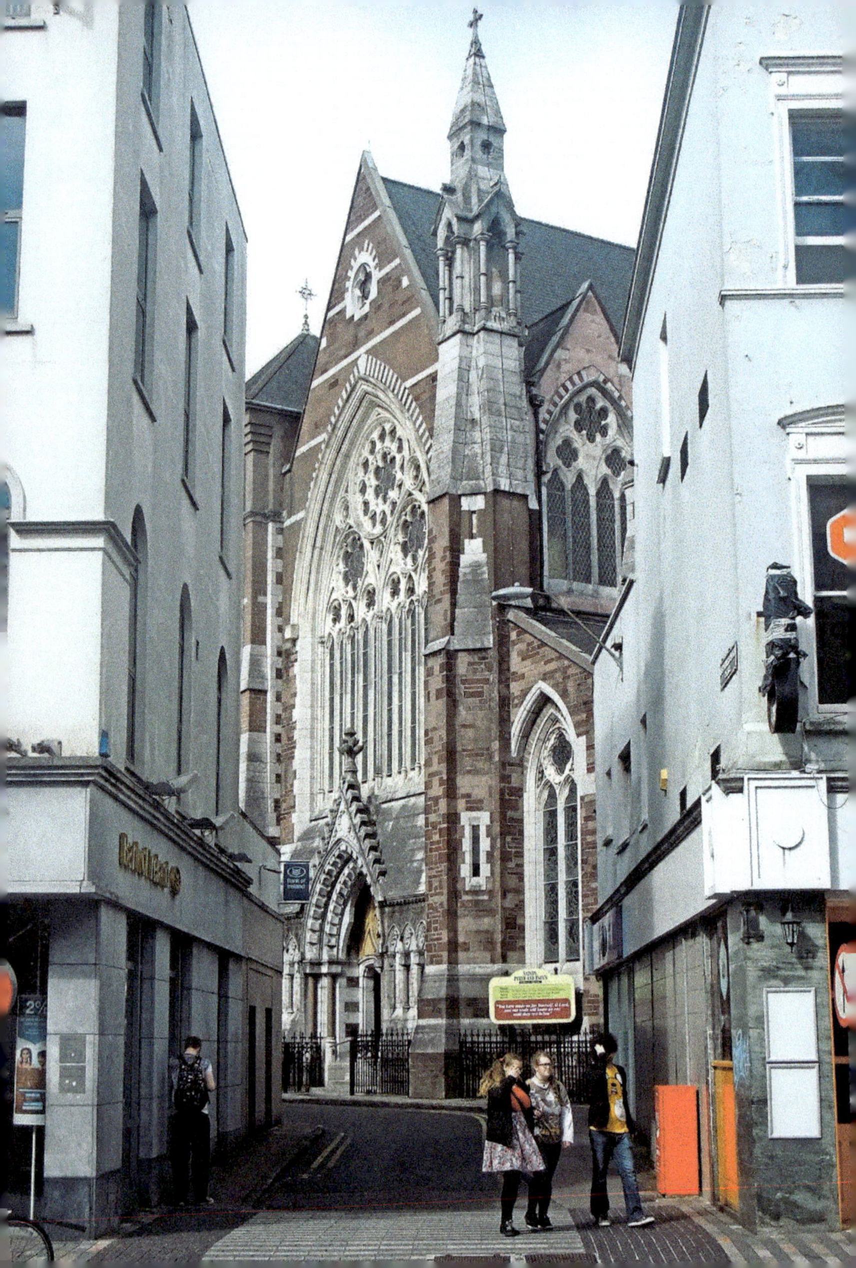

27. ST PETER AND ST PAUL'S CHURCH

For more than 100 years, St Peter and St Paul's Church has stood in a quiet street off Patrick Street. The present building was opened on 29 June 1866 and replaced an older church in decay. Plans for the present-day church were initially proposed in the 1820s. This project did not run according to plan and it was only on the arrival of Father John Murphy to the parish that the project was revitalised under his direction. An architectural competition was arranged and the outright winner was Edward Pugin, the son of eminent English architect Augustus Welby Pugin.

Work on the new Cork church began straightaway. Since the new church had to be built near and west of the old one due to space restrictions in the inner city, the first problem encountered was the marshy ground to be built upon. To resolve the issue, Pugin shortened some of his Gothic designs, including his proposed spire. On 15 August 1859, the foundation stone of the church was laid. The grand altar is of the purest white statuary Carrara marble. The pavements surrounding the altar, and the steps, are all of white Italian vein marble and highly polished. The entire flooring of the church consists of alternative pieces of white and black marble, indicative of the Church of God containing white and black sheep.

28. ENGLISH MARKET

Known as the root market, the English Market was opened in 1788. Today, Corkonians know the English Market under several names: The Princes Street market, the Grand Parade market or some call it 'de market'. By the mid-1800s, it had fallen into a state of disrepair. In 1862, the market was rebuilt under the direction of architect Sir John Benson. The market suffered two fires in 1980 and 1986. After the 1980 fire, the market was renovated at a cost of £500,000 and it was considered a great success – some of the original features were retained. The fire of 1986 caused an estimated £100,000 worth of damage. Nevertheless, the market was again repaired.

29. NATIONAL MONUMENT

The National Monument on the Grand Parade honours the Irish patriots who fought in rebellions. Several lists of names are recorded and it features five statues: Mother Erin; Wolfe tone, the leader of the 1798 rebellion; Fenian leader Peter O'Neill Crowley; Young Irelander Thomas Davis; and United Irishman leader Michael Dwyer. The monument was designed by well-known architect D. J. Coakley and was built by Ellis Coakley. John Francis Davis, a Kilkenny man with a studio in Dublin, sculpted the statues. The Cork Young Ireland society raised funds for its construction. Its foundation stone was laid in 1898, but the finished structure was not unveiled until St Patrick's Day 1906.

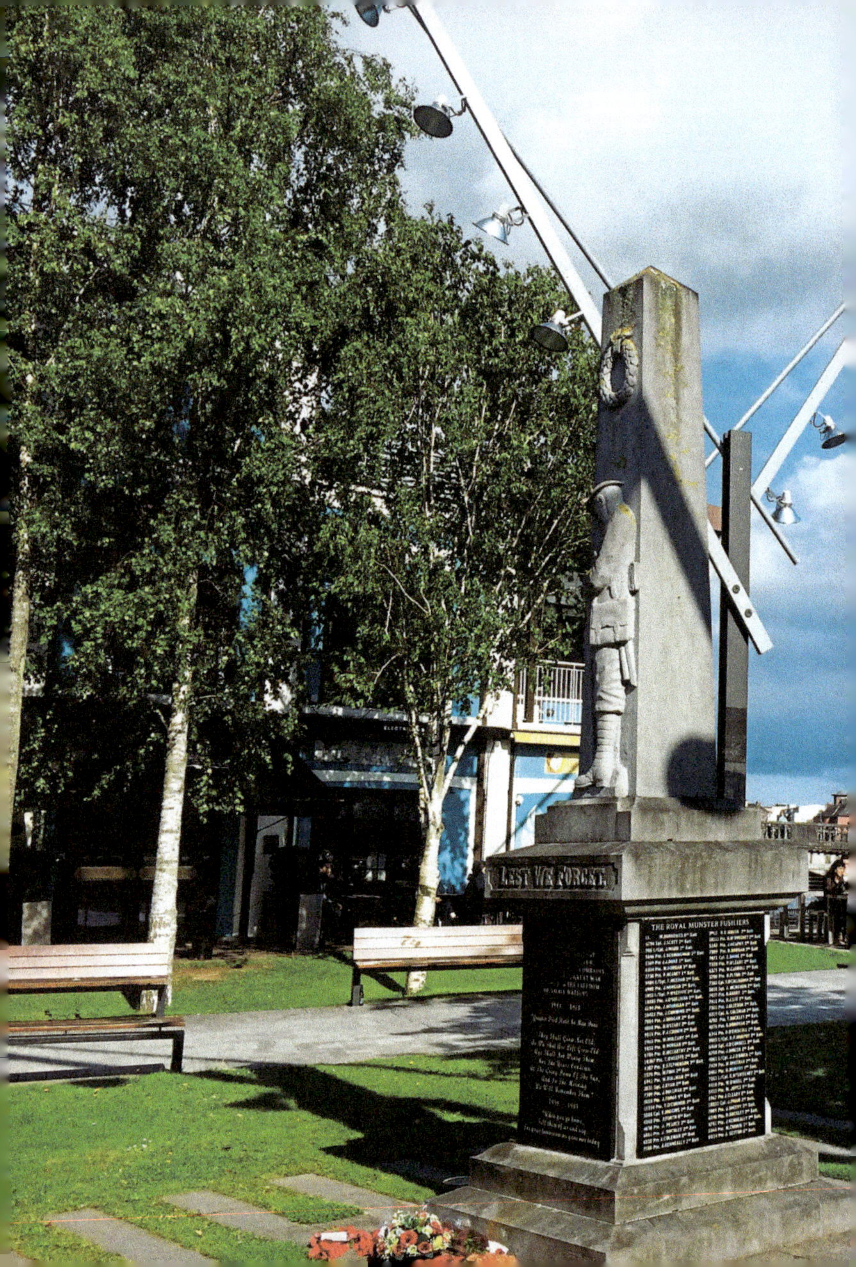
LEST WE FORGET.
THE ROYAL MUNSTER FUSILIERS

30. FIRST WORLD WAR MEMORIAL

At the northern end of the South Mall is a memorial to those Irishmen who died in the First World War. It was erected in 1925 and is one of a few Irish examples. Carved in relief on a modest limestone obelisk, sitting on a plinth is the profile of a Munster Fusiliers soldier in full military uniform, head down, gun at rest. Each November wreaths are laid here to mark the anniversary of the Armistice of 1918. During the First World War, over 2,000 Cork men were killed, some 1,100 of them from Cork City alone. Many of them lie buried with hundreds of thousands of other British soldiers in the cemeteries of northern France and Flanders. Cork got a taste of the horrors of the war when the *Lusitania* was sunk off the Old Head of Kinsale on 8 May 1915.

31. HOLY TRINITY CHURCH

Around 1637, an order of Capuchins arrived in Cork. By the year 1741, a friary was founded behind Sullivan's Quay. Here, they constructed a chapel in 1771 to motivate the large local population to come to church. As time passed and another century began, the brethren was so immense that it was decided by Fr Theobald Matthew OFM CAP to build a larger church on the site, extending into a new area of land. The architect was George Richard Pain. The first foundation stone was laid on 10 October 1832. Shortly after the famine, Cork Corporation decided to pledge an ample sum of money to a memorial for Daniel O'Connell. The memorial in question is the absorbing stained-glass window behind the altar. Finally, on 10 October 1850, eighteen years after the foundation stone was laid, Holy Trinity Church was opened for public worship. However, the question of a spire still remained a problem. Forty years after the opening of the church, the spire and limestone façade were added to remember the birth of Fr Matthew.

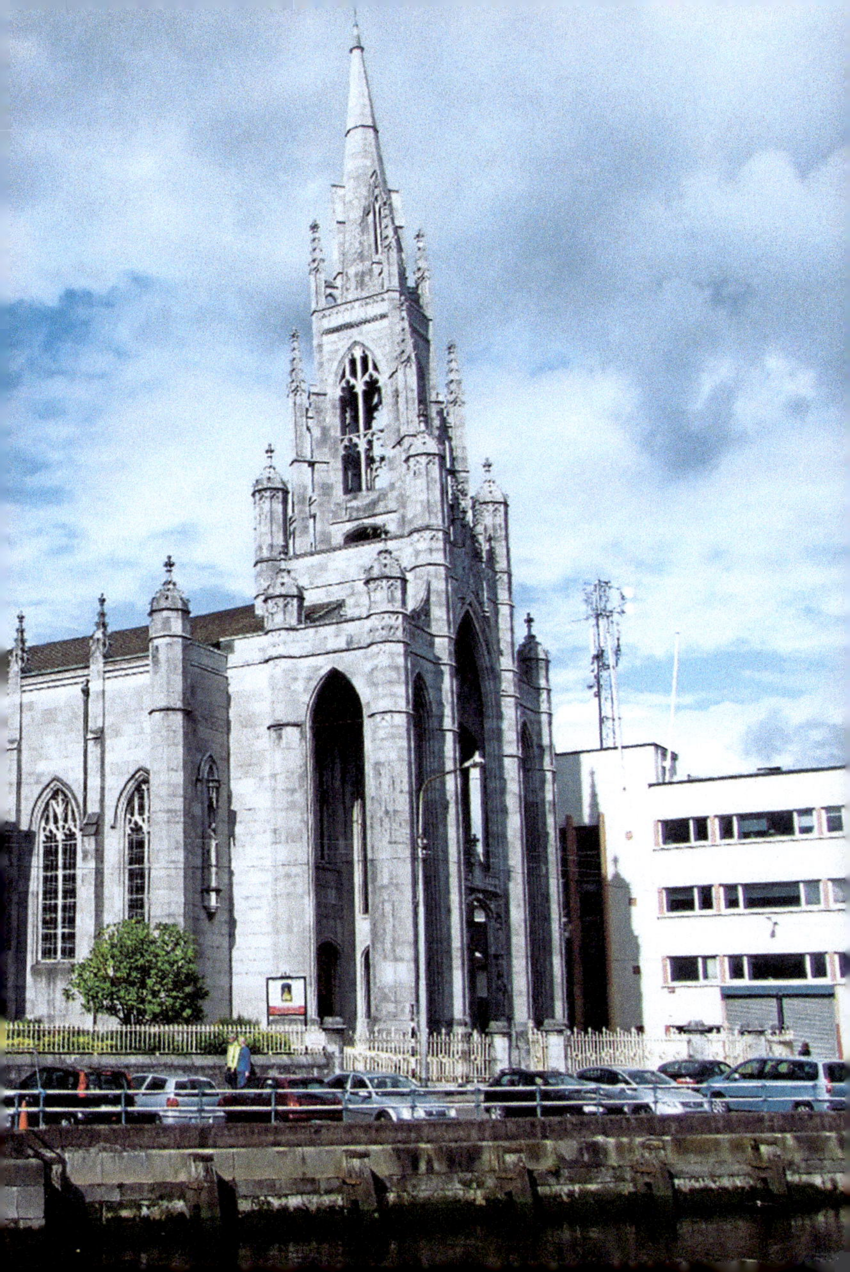

CITY HALL
32. CORK SAVINGS BANK

Private banks, open to landlords and merchants, grew rapidly in the early 1800s, especially during the years of the Napoleonic Wars (1805–14). Banks began to appear in many inland towns and smaller ports where no banks had previously existed. However, after the war, a major recession in the Irish economy occurred, and in the 1820s trade began to grow again. On 2 December 1817, a select committee of Cork's wealthy merchants began to discuss the idea of setting up a savings bank in Cork. The meeting took place in the commercial buildings on the South Mall, now the Imperial Hotel. By the end of the decade, it was decided to build a new building to accommodate the expanding business. In 1839, Sir Thomas Deane resigned from his post as trustee of the bank. He was subsequently chosen to design and oversee the construction of the new building. Lapp's Quay was the chosen site due to its spacious position.

33. PROVINCIAL BANK

The Cork Provincial Bank was built during the years 1863 and 1865 and was acclaimed by many Corkonians on its opening in 1865 as the 'handsomest' public building in Cork. Costing between £15,000 and £20,000, it complemented the older Trustee Saving Bank opposite on Lapp's Quay. The Provincial Bank, of white limestone composition, was designed by Alexander Deane, an uncle of Sir Thomas Deane with William J. Murray, the architect. The ornate style is described as high-Victorian classicism.

The exterior walls are faced with ashlar limestone. On the exterior of the second and upper storey, fluted Corinthian columns divide the space, which support a large pediment in front and two smaller ones on the sides. Semicircular arches exist over the first-floor windows, within which are the coats of arms of Athlone, Derry, Galway, Cork (inset), Wexford and Waterford. Queen Victoria's head is carved on the keystone upon the main frontage.

STATIO BENE FIDA CARINIS

34. CORK CITY HALL

Cork has had a number of city hall sites through the ages but none as grand as the present one. In the age of the Anglo-Norman walled town, civic business was conducted in King's Castle. Business was also conducted in Cork City courthouse in the nineteenth century. In 1883, it was decided by a number of Cork businessmen that the corn exchange should be converted into an exhibition centre – a centre, which, in 1892, became Cork's City Hall.

In December 1920, the premises were burned down by fires attributed to the Black and Tans as retribution for Republican attacks.

A new city hall, by architects Jones and Kelly, was subsequently built. The limestone, like for so many of Cork's buildings, was quarried from nearby Little Island. The building is faced with dressed limestone and incorporates an elegant concert hall. The foundation stone of Cork City Hall was laid by Eamonn de Valera on 9 July 1932. Some departments of Cork Corporation opened in the new building in March 1935, and on 24 April 1935 Cork Corporation held a meeting in the new hall for the first time. The city hall was officially opened on 8 September 1936. Recently, Cork City Council opened a new award-winning extension to the 1930s building.

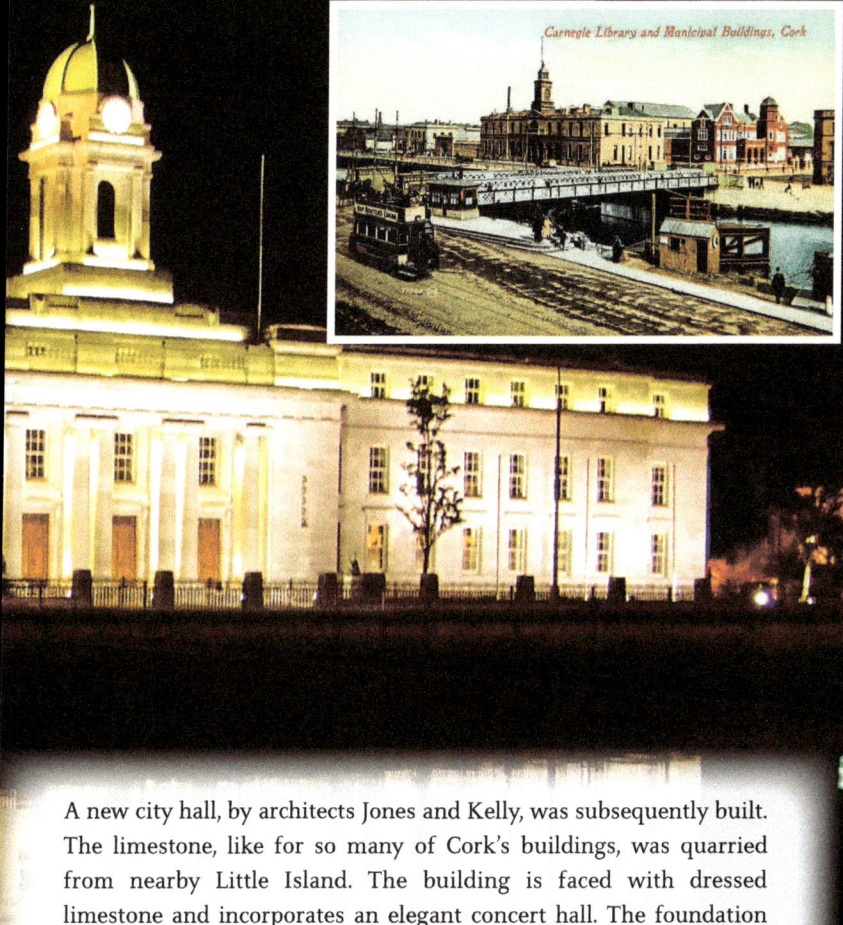

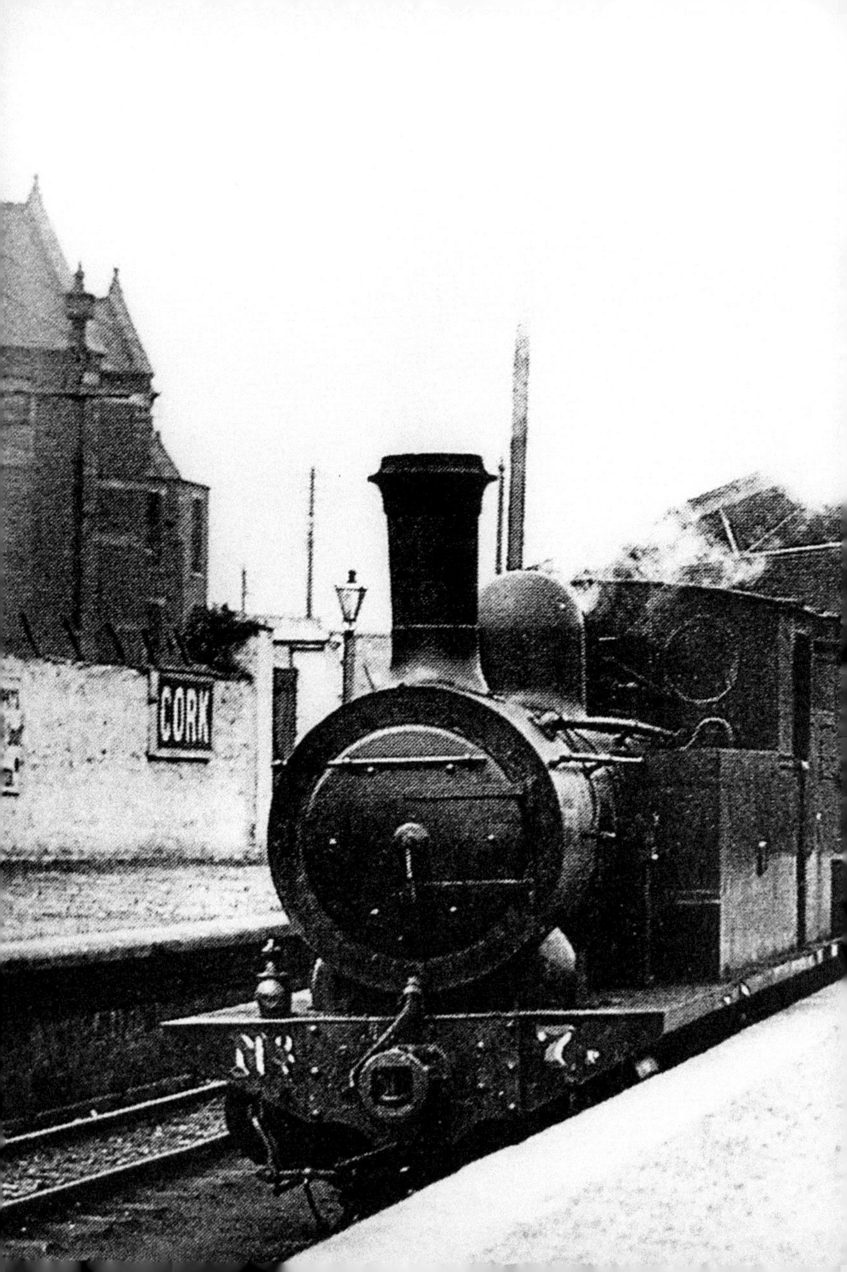
CORK

35. CORK BLACKROCK & PASSAGE RAILWAY LINE

The year 1836 marked the opening of Ireland's first railway, between Dublin and Kingstown. In 1835, the plan for a Cork–Passage railway was first proposed by Cork-based merchant William Parker and Cork solicitor, J. C. Besnard. In that year, Cork Harbour town Passage West had its own dockyard and had become an important port for large deep-sea sailing ships whose cargoes were then transhipped into smaller vessels for the journey upriver to the city. Due to the fact that the construction was taking place during the Great Famine, there was no shortage of labour. The entire length of track between Cork and Passage was in place by April 1850, and within two months the line was opened for passenger traffic. The site of the second Cork terminus lies opposite the National Sculpture Factory.

36. GASWORKS

By 1823, numerous towns and cities throughout Britain were lit by gas. Gaslight cost up to 75 per cent less than oil lamps or candles, which helped to accelerate its development. By 1859, gas lighting was to be found all over Britain and around 1,000 gasworks had sprung up to meet the demand for the new fuel. In 1825, the Cork Wide Street Commissioners, a municipal planning agency of sorts, entered into an arrangement with the United Gas Co. of London to provide Cork City with gas lighting between the hours of sunset and sunrise, with each gas lamp to provide light equivalent to that of twelve mould tallow candles. The site today is now occupied by the national offices of Bord Gáis.

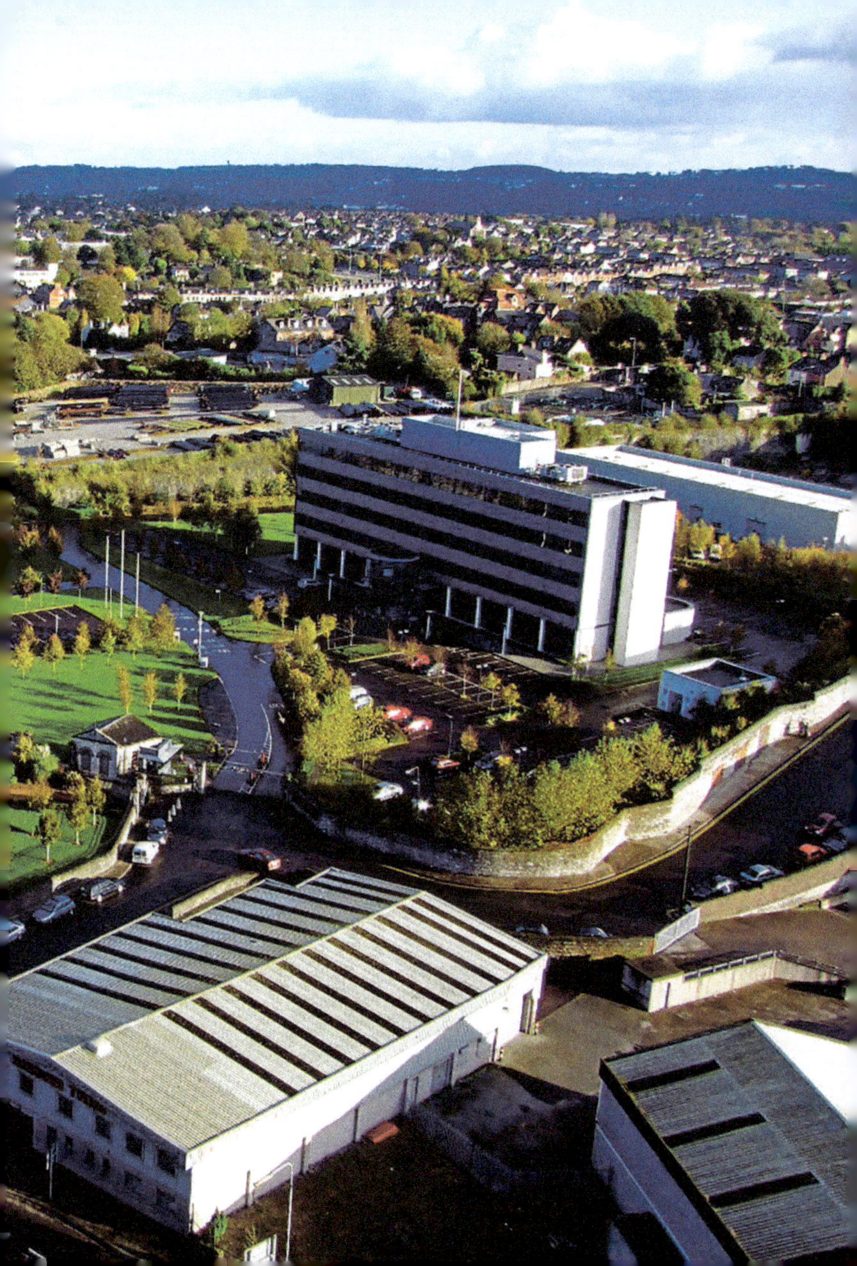

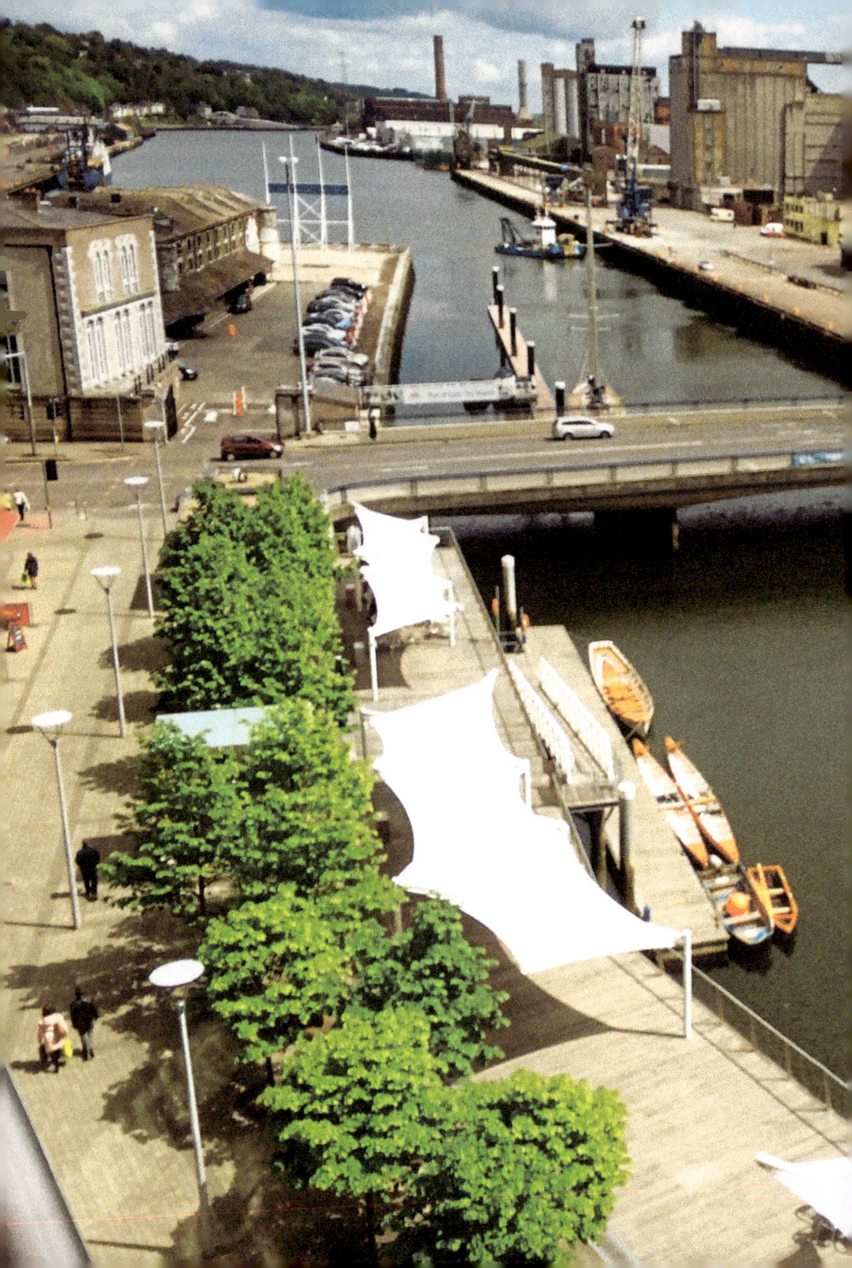

37. DOCKS

Ever since Viking times, boats of all different shapes and sizes have been coming in and out of Cork's riverine and harbour region, continuing a very long legacy of trade. One hundred years ago, considerable tonnage could navigate the North Channel as far as St Patrick's Bridge, and on the South Channel as far as Parliament Bridge. In the late 1800s, the port of Cork was the leading commercial port of Ireland. The export of pickled pork, bacon, butter, corn, porter, and spirits was considerable. The manufactures of the city were brewing, distilling and coach-building, which were all carried on extensively. There were many large establishments in the timber trade, also many in which salt provisions were cured, and several tanneries, which produced leather of the choicest quality. There were also some salt, lime and chemical works.

38. FORD WORKS

In November 1916, Ford made an offer to purchase the freehold of the Cork Park Grounds and considerable land adjoining the river near the Marina. Ford, Cork Corporation and the Harbour Commissioners entered into formal negotiations. The company acquired approximately 130 acres of land, which also had a river frontage. The factory gave employment to at least 2,000 adult males, paid the minimum wage of 1s per hour.

The plant being laid down by the company was specially designed for the manufacture of an Agricultural Motor Tractor, well known as the 'fordson', a 22 horsepower, four-cylinder tractor, working with kerosene or paraffin, adaptable either for ploughing or as a portable engine arranged for driving machinery by belt drive. The demand for such tractors was universal and great. Large areas could be brought under food production with the minimum of expense and labour. The Cork factory was to provide 'Fordsons' to local, regional and national farmers and further afield on the Continent.

Ford's Works, Cork.

THE IMPROVED
FORDSON
TRACTOR ARE

>>> Manufactured a[nd] Built Exclusively in Cork. In their latest devel[op]ment, there is nothing else offering so good valu[e] judged on the point either of first cost, running co[st] or maintenance charges.

The New INDUSTRIAL MODEL
works wonders in the reduction of road-haulage costs, especially for loads of 6 to 8 tons.

The Local Fordson Deale[r] Will Gladly Demonstra[te] The Capabilities of Eith[er] Model, in Your Own D[is]trict, But At His Own Co[st] and Responsibility.

FORDSON Users have access Everywhere to FORDSON Facilities, with definite, fixed and low charges for every replacement, every repair.

AGRICULTURAL MODEL
WITH CLEATS **£140**
WITH SPADE LUGS **£143**
AT WORKS, CORK.

HENRY FORD & SO[NS] LIMITED, CORK, IRELAND

The Marina, Cork.

39. THE MARINA

Cork's marina, originally called the Navigation Wall, was completed in 1761. In 1820, Cork Harbour Commissioners formed and purchased a locally built dredger. The dredger deposited silt from the river into wooden barges, which were then towed ashore. The silt was redeposited behind the Navigation Wall. During the Great Famine, deepening of the river created jobs for 1,000 men who worked on creating the Navigation Wall's road – The Marina. The environs is also home to three large rowing clubs: the Lee Rowing Club, founded in 1850, which is the second oldest club in the country; Shandon Boat Club, founded in 1875; and Cork Boat Club, founded in 1899 by members of Dolphin Swimming Club – all of which ply the waters of the river regularly and who have annual regattas.

Blackrock Castle, Cork.

40. BLACKROCK CASTLE

The imposing Blackrock Castle is the third structure on the site. The citizens of Cork built Blackrock Castle in 1582 to safeguard ships against pirates who would come into the harbour and steal their vessels. The fort, which was then a circular tower, was used as a beacon light from a turf fire to guide shipping. The building has been destroyed by fire twice – in 1722 and 1827 – and rebuilt. In the eighteenth century, admiralty courts were held at Blackrock Castle to oversee fishery rights. It was the court's job to also organise an important ceremony called 'Throwing the Dart'. This was a rite by which the Mayor of Cork threw a metre-long dart into the water of Cork Harbour in order to show his authority over the port and harbour. This is a function still carried out by the Lord Mayor of Cork. The castle now hosts an interactive astronomy centre.

WESTERN QUARTER
41. MERCY HOSPITAL

The Mercy Hospital was once the site of the old Mansion House. The stone porch, the entrance and the magnificent mahogany staircase is still standing, and one can view the beautiful frescoed ceilings on the upper floors. The Mansion House was built in 1767 and cost £3,793, with large, expensive dining and sitting rooms, designed by the Italian architect Davis Dukart. In March 1842, the bill was £1,000 for repairs and furnishings to make it fit for a mayoral residence. On 21 June 1844, the Corporation granted a seventy-five-year lease of the building to two Cork priests, Revd Michael O'Sullivan and Revd Michael Scully, who created St Vincent's Seminary at the house. On St Patrick's Day 1857, the Sisters of Mercy embarked on creating the Mercy Hospital at the site. Forty beds were ready on the first day but only six patients were admitted. Today, the hospital has 314 beds and employs approximately 1,000 staff.

42. WISE'S DISTILLERY

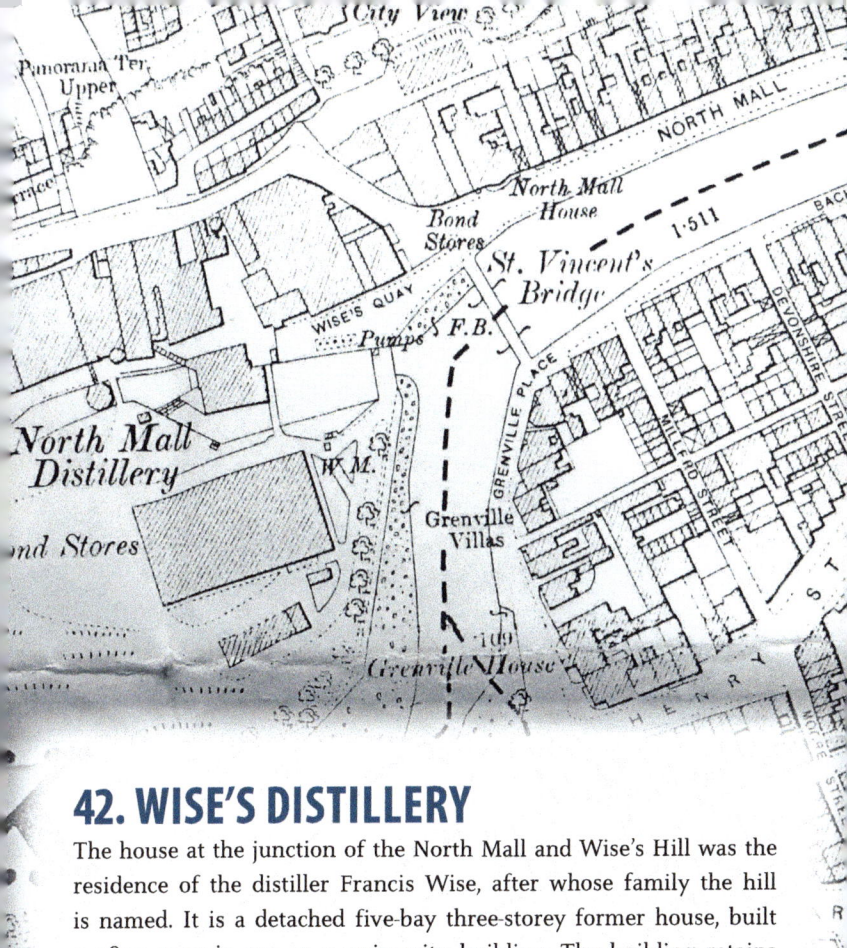

The house at the junction of the North Mall and Wise's Hill was the residence of the distiller Francis Wise, after whose family the hill is named. It is a detached five-bay three-storey former house, built *c.* 1800, now in use as a university building. The building retains interesting features and materials, such as the timber sliding sash windows, wrought-iron lamp bracket arch and interior fittings. The North Mall distillery was established on Reilly's Marsh around 1779, and by 1802 the Wise brothers were running the firm. Whiskey production was another significant industry in Cork from the late eighteenth century.

St. Vincent's Church, Su

43. ST VINCENT'S CHURCH

The site of the church was donated to the Vincentian Fathers by Miss Mary MacSwiney of Sunday's Well. The plans for the church were prepared by Sir John Benson, whose other works included the building of thirty bridges in County Cork, the reconstruction of the North Gate Bridge and the city's Athenaeum, which was later converted into the Opera House, just to mention a few.

The foundation stone was laid on 24 October 1851. On 4 November 1853, disaster struck. The walls were built and the church was partially roofed when a powerful storm swept away the roof and stonework. This provoked the sympathy and charitable support of the people of Cork and many friends in the south of Ireland. The church was soon rebuilt and opened. Among the many beautiful attractions of this church are the seven double-panel windows that adorn the aisles south and north – made in Munich by the best stained-glass manufacturers of that time, Messrs Mayer & Co., Munich.

44. CORK CITY GAOL

The construction of Cork City Gaol commenced in 1821 and on 17 August 1824, the first prisoners were incarcerated. Fast-forward 100 years and, amid a backdrop of the Irish Free State Civil War, the gaol was used to imprison members of the Irish Republican Army. Eminent examples of internees include many members of Cumann na mBan, especially one patriotic Cork woman, Mary Bowles; Countess Constance Markievicz, famous republican and member of the first Dáil Eireann in 1919; and Frank O'Connor who went on to become an eminent Irish writer after his release.

The aftermath of the War of Independence in the late 1910s culminated in a treaty between the proclaimed Irish government and the British government and a subsequent civil war between Irish patriots. Subsequently, many anti-treaty followers were interned in camps and prisons throughout Ireland, including in the gaol in Sunday's Well. In October 1923, a major hunger strike was begun in Mountjoy Gaol in Dublin by prisoners. In Cork, nearly 100 prisoners went on hunger strike and it was decided by Cork Corporation, for the safety of internees, that the unconditional release of the majority of anti-treaty prisoners be passed. The drawings from the imprisoned men are preserved on the gaol cell walls and can still be seen today on a guided tour.

45. DALY'S BRIDGE

Built in 1926, Daly's Bridge spans a section of the river that is surrounded by greenery. Fitzgerald's Park is on the south side and several landscaped gardens are on the north side. Prior to 1926, it had been suggested many times that a footbridge should be built in the locality to enhance the area. It was therefore decided by the corporation to go halves on building a bridge with James Daly, a butter merchant in the city. A decision was made to construct a suspension bridge, which would be supported at intervals across the river with the aid of anchored cables. A pedestrian walkway consisting of timber planks was also constructed. The building contract was awarded to a London-based steel company owned by David R. Bell. It is more commonly known as the 'Shaky Bridge', attaining the name due to the fact that a large number of people used the bridge to go to and from Gaelic matches in the Mardyke and it would shake as a result.

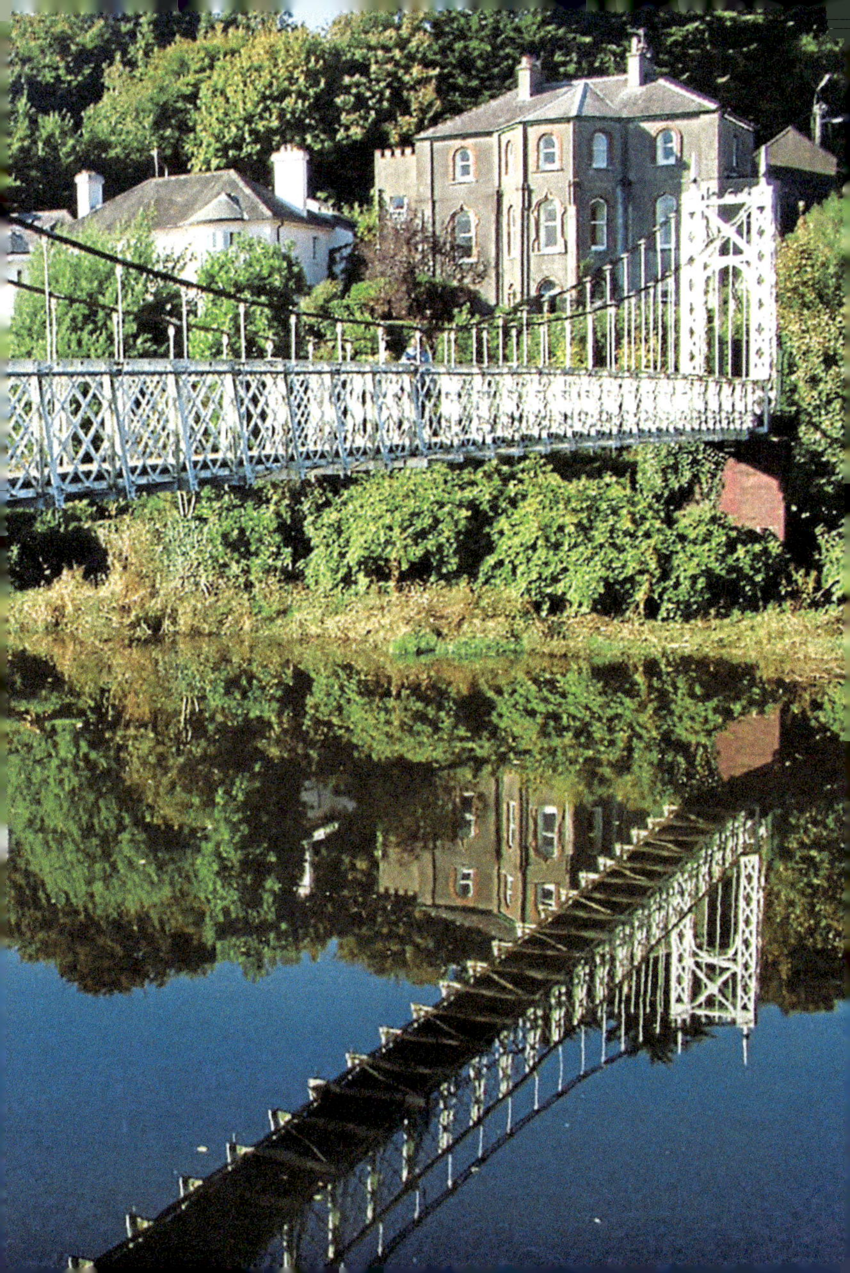

46. SUNDAY'S WELL BOATING AND TENNIS CLUB

Sunday's Well Boating and Tennis Club was founded in 1899, shortly after a successful July Sunday's Well Regatta and Water Carnival had been held on the Lee. The club was formed by some of the regatta committee organisers, who were boating and tennis enthusiasts. The committee then leased a plot of ground off the Mardyke Walk alongside the river and that is the ground the club occupies today. As a club, Sunday's Well is fortunate in that it can boast having a comprehensive range of annals dating from its foundation right up to present times. It was uniquely linked with the Cork International Exhibition of 1902/03 and the present clubhouse was built by the Exhibition Committee for visiting dignitaries, which included King Edward VII and Queen Alexandra.

In 1904, the club took possession of the clubhouse. Sunday's Well had, in addition to its magnificent new clubhouse, five excellently laid-out and perfectly manicured grass courts. These, set in peaceful and beautiful surroundings, thus became the pride of the country. Throughout the summer, the courts were constantly used from morning to night, except on band promenade days, which were held regularly during the summer months in front of the clubhouse.

47. LIFETIME LAB

Dating from the nineteenth and twentieth centuries, the buildings stand on the Waterworks site today, but water has been supplied to the city of Cork from the site since the 1760s. A foundation stone commemorates the building of the first pump house on Lee Road in the late eighteenth century. In 1768, Nicholas Fitton was elected to carry out the construction work for the new water supply plan. The waterwheel and pump sent the unfiltered river water to an open reservoir called the 'City Basin'. Officially opened in October 2005, the Lifetime Lab, a Cork City Council initiative funded by the European Free Trade Association, was a welcome move in protecting and reinvigorating Cork's heritage stock. The old Waterworks on Lee Road has been converted into a 'lab' where visitors of all ages can enjoy a modern interactive exhibition, steam plant, beautifully restored buildings, children's playground and marvellous views over the Lee Fields.

ASCENDING THE NORTH-EAST
48. AUDLEY PLACE

This view from the top is a much-loved, often photographed view and has been captured in a sketch by historian Charles Smith in 1750, a painting by John Butts in the 1760s (now on display in the Crawford Art Gallery) and a photographic postcard in the early nineteenth century. The early depictions show the early growth of Blackpool as an industrial hub in the city, with its myriad chimneys reflecting the many tanneries and distilleries in the area. The postcard shows a young St Mary and St Anne's North Cathedral and echoes the social and physical change of nineteenth-century Victorian Cork.

49. COLLINS BARRACKS

Built between 1801 and 1806 and designed initially by John Gibson, Collins Barracks was once called Royal or Cork Barracks. It was constructed as a response to the huge overcrowding of British Army personnel in Elizabeth Fort and its subsidiary, Cat Barracks. Occupying 37 acres, the Georgian square became the largest military parade ground in Europe. It was described in contemporary sources as conveniently adapted to accommodate 156 officers and 1,994 men and stabling for 232 horses. The grounds for parade and exercise were spacious and there was a hospital capable of receiving 120 patients.

The eminent clock tower was built in 1852. The Cork Dublin railway

The Barracks, Cork.

tunnel runs directly beneath the barracks and after its construction had to be guarded twenty-four hours a day during times of unrest. Schooling was provided in the barracks for children of NCOs. A cemetery, industries and enterprises developed around the barracks. In 1921, Major Bernard Montgomery handed over the barracks to Óglaigh na hÉireann Commandant Seán Murray. On 10 August 1922, the barrack buildings were burnt down by anti-treaty forces. The buildings were restored and the barracks were renamed Michael Collins Barracks after the War of Independence leader and head of the pro-Treaty and Irish Free State Army. In 1939, the barracks became the home of the First Southern Division, a position it still holds.

50. METROPOLE HOTEL

In 1876, brothers Stuart and Thomas Musgrave opened a grocery store on North Main Street in Cork. They were aged twenty-five and eighteen and had moved to Cork from County Leitrim. The business incorporated in 1894 as Musgrave Brothers Ltd, with a charter to retail and wholesale sugar, coffee, tea, spices, fruit, olive oil, and other foodstuffs. The company also ran a bakery and confectionary and was listed as a mineral water manufacturer, iron and hardware merchant, druggist, fish and ice merchant, stationer and haberdasher.

At the same time, the Musgrave Brothers built and ran Cork's iconic Metropole Hotel, as well as a sweet factory and a laundry. The first Musgrave grocery relocated to larger premises at No. 84 Grand Parade. In 1925, the company moved to a large new premises on Cornmarket Street. By this time, the business was almost exclusively wholesale. Musgrave now serves more than 3,000 stores in Ireland, the UK and Spain, and has annual wholesale turnover of €4.4 billion and global retail sales of €6.7 billion.

51. ST PATRICK'S CHURCH

In the 1830s, a mass house stood on the Strand Road in the vicinity of the future site of Cork's Kent railway station. The church was located near a brick factory and thus attained the name 'Brickfield Chapel'. A family named O'Mahony were wealthy merchants in the North Parish and had woollen mills in Blackpool and Blarney. Within this family was a son named Francis Sylvester who was chaplain in the North Presentation Convent and helped out in the nearby Fever Hospital. The O'Mahonys were interested in financing a new church, primarily near Brickfield Chapel. The design of the church was given to a young architect named George Pain. He chose a Grecian style but had to be satisfied instead with a Corinthian style of architecture. The church was supposed to be finished in 1838. Five years after the proposed finishing date, the parishioners were still having meetings to try to raise funds for the completion of the front façade. The church was finally opened for public worship on 1 July 1848 and was dedicated to St Patrick.

ABOUT THE AUTHOR

For over twenty years Kieran has actively promoted Cork's heritage with its various communities and people. He has led and continues to lead successful heritage initiatives through his community talks, city and county school heritage programmes, walking tours, newspaper articles, books and through his heritage consultancy business. For the past seventeen years Kieran has written a local heritage column in the *Cork Independent* on the history, geography and its intersection of modern-day life in communities in Cork City and county. He holds a PhD in Cultural Geography from University College Cork and has interests in ideas of landscape, collective memory, narrative and identity structures.

Kieran is the author of seventeen books. In June 2009 and May 2014, Kieran was elected as a local government councillor (Independent) to Cork City Council. He is also a member of the EU's Committee of the Regions. More on Kieran's work can be seen at www.corkheritage.ie and www.kieranmccarthy.ie.

ACKNOWLEDGEMENTS

I would like to thank Cork City Library, Cork Museum and Cork City Council for access to old images and maps. The photographs are my own, taken over many years. I would also like to thank Rochelle Stanley of Amberley Publishing for her courtesy and professionalism.